Jean Lee

by Bronwyn Miller
illustrated by Arvis Stewart

Practice Decodable 58

Mc Graw Hill Education

Bothell, WA • Chicago, IL • Columbus, OH • New York, NY

MHEonline.com

Send all inquiries to:
McGraw-Hill Education
8787 Orion Place
Columbus, OH 43240

ISBN: 978-0-02-145387-0
MHID: 0-02-145387-X

Printed in China

8 9 10 11 12 DSS 27 26 25 24 23

I am Jean Lee, a weather person.
I am on the screen.

Is the wind heading east or west?
Will we feel hot or cold?

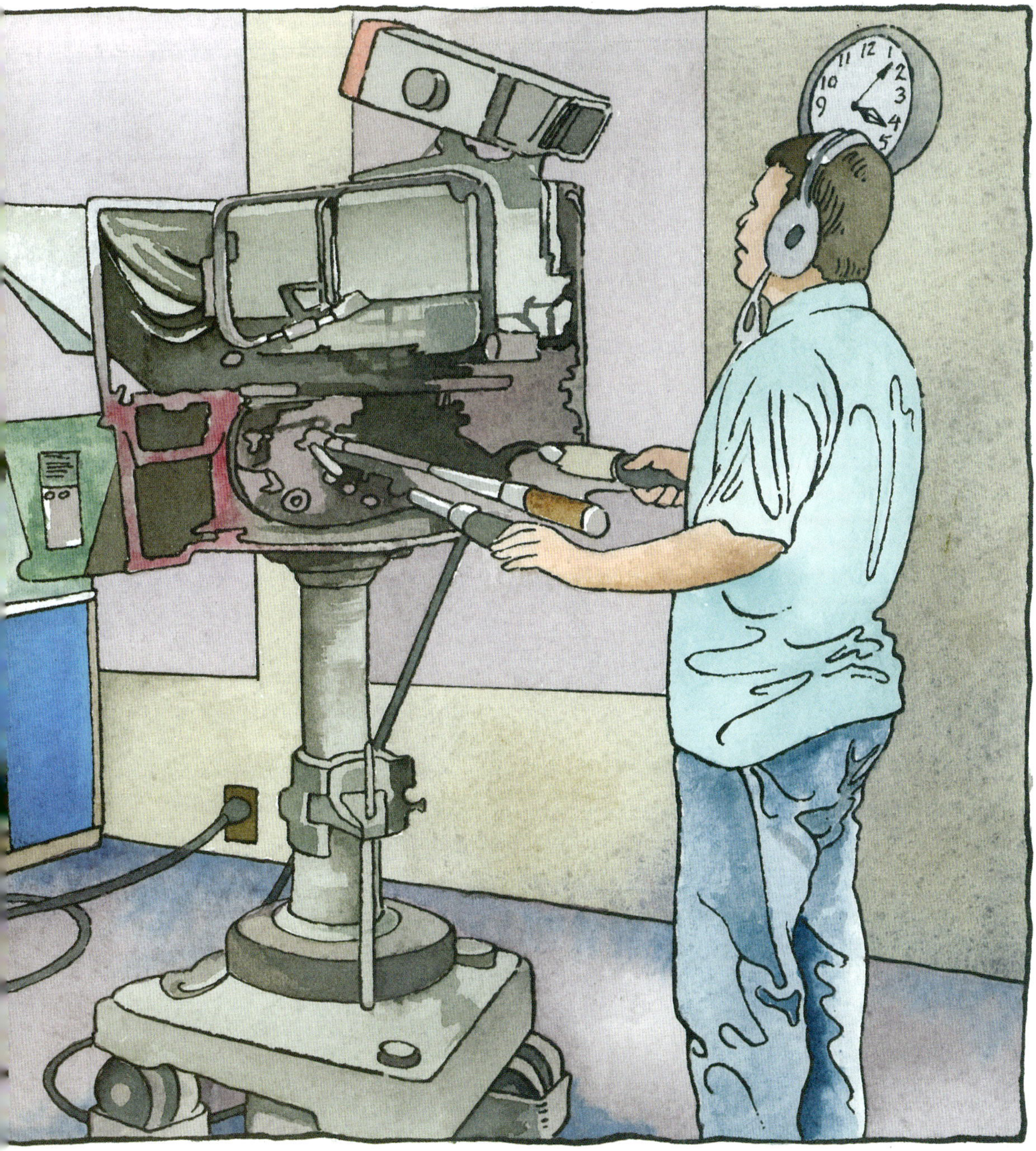

I tell these two things.

If the weather is nice, I am glad.

In nice weather, each fan seems upbeat.
Fans wave on the street.

In bad weather, fans disappear.
If I see them, they seem mad.

Please remember, I just tell the weather.

I do not make it!